RAW·CHOCOLATE·MAKING·
WITH·CHOCOMAMA

RAW·CHOCOLATE·MAKING·

WITH·CHOCOMAMA

How to make this delicious, vegan superfood in your own kitchen

Sue Frisby

Copyright © 2021 Sue Frisby

All rights reserved.

ISBN: 9798734465790

This book is dedicated to my chocolate teacher, Amy Levin

CONTENTS

· Introduction 1
· Here's The Plan 3
· Getting Started 6

PART·ONE

RAW CHOCOLATE MAKING: THEORY AND PHILOSOPHY

· What Is Raw Chocolate (or rather, What Do *I* Mean By Raw Chocolate)? 13
· What Are The Benefits Of Raw Chocolate? 15
· The Beauty of Homemade, Handmade Chocolate 19
· The Raw Chocolate Culture 22
· Let's Compare Raw Chocolate with Conventional Chocolate 29
· How to Work Out Cacao (Or Cocoa) Percentage 32
· Other Sweeteners 34

PART·TWO

RAW CHOCOLATE MAKING: THE PRACTICE

· Equipment and Tools You'll Need 42
· Ingredients 48
· Preparing Your Chocolate Making Space 54
· Preparing Your Ingredients 58
· Simple Raw (Untempered) Chocolate 62
· Candied Inclusions: #1 Maple-Candied Orange Peel 66
· Orange Chocolates 69
· Tempered Raw Chocolate 72
· How to Temper Raw Chocolate 75
· Candied Inclusions: #2 Coconut Crispies 82
· Coconut Crispies in Tempered Raw Chocolate 86
· Chocolate Trouble: Troubleshooting 90
· Acknowledgements, Credits, References, Index 96

Quetzalcoatl, the much-loved Mesoamerican God of Life, Light and Wisdom

According to ancient myth, Quetzalcoatl, also known as the Feathered Serpent, brought cacao beans from paradise. He gave them to the people so they might be well-nourished, becoming wise, and accomplished in the arts.

INTRODUCTION

CHOCOLATE!

There is something very special about chocolate. Most of us would agree. And for most of us it is a joyous indulgence.

We love it!

As you probably know, chocolate can be so much more than just an indulgence.

When made properly, chocolate can be one of the most nourishing foodstuffs around. It's full of amazing levels of nutrients in its pure form.

This is what we are searching for when we eat chocolate - chemicals that make us feel good, like serotonin; minerals that deeply relax us, like magnesium; and energy boosters, like iron.

We associate chocolate with love, giving it as a gift to those who matter to us. So doesn't it make sense when we discover that it is food for the heart, heart-healthy food?

Those of us who eat chocolate can significantly cut our risk of a heart attack, according to a range of research[1]. It contains high levels of antioxidants that ease blood pressure and help good circulation.

These anti-oxidants also improve brain function. It is rich in healthy fatty acids that are good for the brain as well.

So it will be no surprise that it has been hailed as a superfood.

However, I am talking about a particular kind of chocolate. This is *raw chocolate* - made from unroasted cacao beans - which I have been making professionally for many years.

Raw chocolate is made from some of the most healthy and most delicious ingredients around. And what is amazing is that you can make raw chocolate in the comfort of your own kitchen.

So why is raw chocolate so healthy, so good for us to eat?

That special something that we know is there, that we are reaching for when we eat this lovely thing, that special something is the raw cacao bean – the **source** of all chocolate.

Highly processed chocolate is but a poor substitute for the real thing.

Chocolate made with gently-treated ingredients maintains its integrity and we find we can at last be truly satisfied.

So, are you tempted to learn how to make your own chocolate with delicious natural ingredients?

I hope so, and by the end of the book you will have your own personal, unique relationship with this most special gift from Mother Earth.

HERE'S THE PLAN

In this book I will show you how to make the most delicious raw chocolate imaginable ~ handmade, homemade, real chocolate in your own kitchen, using simple equipment and high quality natural and organic ingredients.

CHOCOLATE VALUES

In Part One, we will look at some of the theory, philosophy and values behind raw chocolate. I will explain what I mean by *raw chocolate*.

We'll look at what makes it so wonderful and what a beautiful thing it is to make chocolate by hand.

We'll take a glimpse into the inspiring culture behind the raw chocolate movement, where you'll find the high standards and dedication that typify artisan raw chocolate makers.

CACAO PERCENTAGE

We'll look at the specific differences between unroasted and roasted chocolate and what is meant by cacao percentage.

This is useful if you want to create a chocolate bar with a particular level of cacao.

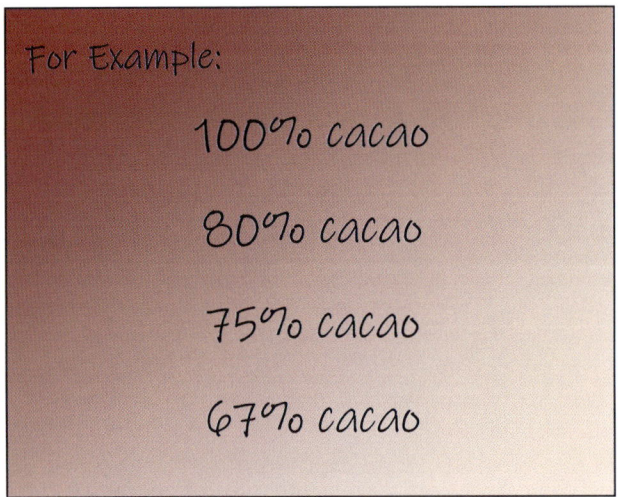

You can control the cacao strength of your chocolate

THE PRACTICE

In Part Two, I'll be sharing with you my prime recipe which will give you a solid foundation for all of your raw chocolate making projects. Its simplicity is inspiring and the results will delight you.

Straight away you will be able to make chocolate that is pure and deeply satisfying.

When you are ready for more you will be able to use this recipe to go on to create a myriad of wonderful variations as you play with flavours and textures.

Textures are wonderful in raw chocolate

The chocolate you will be making is healthy, vegan, without gluten or refined white sugar.

It will be the very best dark, 75% chocolate.

Its deep rich taste really hits the spot, yet it's without the bitterness often associated with commercial dark chocolate.

EQUIPMENT

We will start by looking at the equipment that you'll need, much of which you'll probably already have or will be able to buy easily at a low cost.

INGREDIENTS

You will discover the special ingredients that combine to make amazing chocolate that is deep in flavour and full of vitality.

The root of it all is, of course, raw cacao.

SETTING UP

You will learn the raw chocolate making process, step by step, starting with simple untempered chocolate.

Home chocolate making set-up

But even before that, I will take you through everything you need to know about setting up a chocolate making session – how to prepare your space and how to prepare your ingredients. That way you will have confidence straight away that you've got everything to hand, everything is ready for you and you are ready for chocolate!

CHOCOLATE INCLUSIONS

Once I have shown you how to make untempered chocolate, I will be sharing with you a great method of sweetening orange peel to add to it – it's delicious and has the bonus of the most wonderful smell wafting through your kitchen for hours!

TEMPERING

Then I will show you how to temper raw chocolate, looking first at what that means. Tempering will lift your creations to impressive new levels, creating shine, snap and stability in chocolate.

By the end of this book you will be able to temper chocolate like the professionals do.

MORE CHOCOLATE INCLUSIONS

What wonderful things might you put in your tempered chocolate? To start you off, I will be sharing with you a really great way of transforming dried coconut into maple-flavoured crispies that will be so more-ish you will have to be careful you don't eat them before you get the chance to add them to your chocolate. Together with chocolate they create such a harmonious partnership.

HELP!

Finally, I will go through some common problems you may run into as you make your chocolate, so that hopefully you can avoid them. Or if not, know what to do next time. You will be pleased to know that chocolate is a forgiving medium to work with. Very little is ever wasted!

Handmade chocolate is a wonderful thing

CREATING BY HAND

This book will be all about making **handmade chocolate**. We will be enjoying the process of working with our hands, with these wonderful ingredients. Chocolate making in this way can be mesmerizing, meditative and restoring to the spirit. Your kitchen, even your whole house, will smell delicious!

GETTING STARTED

WHO IS THIS BOOK FOR?

This book is for anyone who wants to explore *real* chocolate.

This means chocolate that is as close as possible to its source, the cacao bean. Unlike a lot of commercial chocolate and its derivatives, real chocolate contains a high level of actual chocolate in it!

A love of chocolate may have brought you here, or a desire to make natural, delicious treats for your family. You may have young children and you want to give them only the very best, highly nutritious snacks.

You or your loved ones may be vegan, eat a raw food diet, or have other particular dietary needs.

CHOCOLATE ADDICTS REJOICE!

Maybe you have chocolate cravings and want to satisfy them with real chocolate. You're in good company!

You might love playing around with your food and trying new things.

You might be considering a natural chocolate business.

You might be inspired by *chocolate* itself - this food that is so sensual to work with.

Whatever brought you here, if you love chocolate and you love natural food, if you enjoy being creative and experimental, you're in the right place.

What brought me to this wonderful subject was a love for chocolate, but it was coupled with a realisation as to how addictive and how unsatisfying conventional chocolate could be for me.

When I heard, in 2008, that there was something called *raw chocolate* my ears pricked up and I instinctively knew there was something very interesting afoot!

I have not been disappointed!

CHOCOLATE AS ART, CRAFT AND SCIENCE

As you go through this book, you will be embarking on something that is a craft, an art and a science. You may very well find you want to explore deeper into one or more of those aspects.

Like crafting the perfect chocolate bar, or using chocolate in a way nobody has done before, or becoming an expert in hand-tempering.

SOME BASICS

In order to begin, you will, of course, need the use of a kitchen, along with certain equipment, including a fridge, and a stove. You will need a place to store your chocolate, safe from the unwanted attention of your pets. And don't forget - dogs can't tolerate chocolate.

We will look more closely at the equipment you will need later on.

Before you begin your chocolate making, you will need to clear a designated area. Give yourself plenty of space to organise your equipment, prepare and weigh out your ingredients.

We will look at how to prepare your chocolate making space in more detail later.

BEWARE MOISTURE

The ideal chocolate making environment is cool and dry ~ which is strange seeing as how cacao is a jungle plant!

You need to keep moisture away from your chocolate, particularly if you are tempering. Moisture causes chocolate to seize: in other words, form clumps. Then you won't be able to use it for its original purpose.

You may very well turn your love of chocolate into a business, like I did. You'll then discover there's a growing market for it, full of adventurous, enthusiastic, artisan producers.

However, if this happens, don't despair. You might create something unexpected! Like delicious ganache. And end up going in a completely different direction.

Wonderful things can come from so-called mistakes, of course.

I created some rather delicious truffles from playing around with seized chocolate, after I had invited ideas from a raw chocolate Facebook group I am part of.

There is an encouraging community out there!

You will want some undisturbed time to learn this new skill. Put aside a few hours to make your first batch of chocolate so that you can fully immerse yourself in the experience. There are wonderful smells and luscious sights to enjoy, and it's all very tactile. Once you get familiar with the process it could well become a meditative activity for you, that you find yourself relaxing deeply into.

I love my chocolate-making sessions and it is my hope that this book will enable you to enjoy making raw chocolate as much as I do.

Whiskey Truffle mixture ~ mistakes can turn out to be very satisfying!

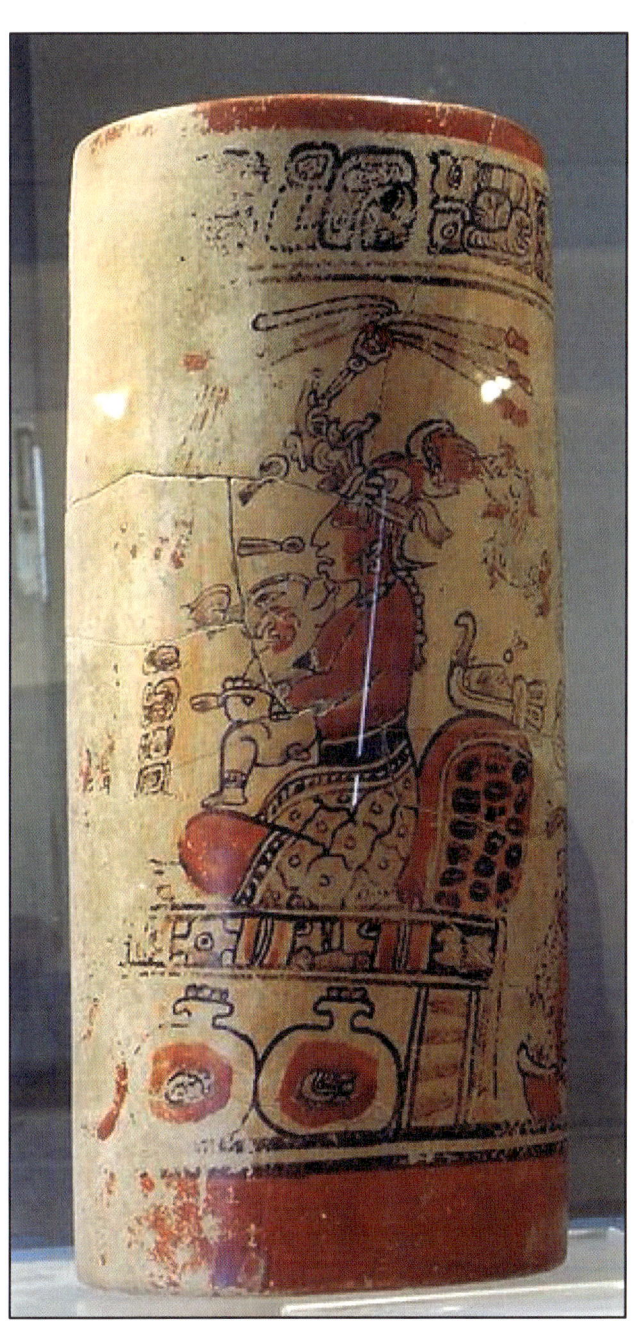

Ancient Mayan Chocolate Drinking Vessel

Owned by a lord of Naranjo, a pre-Columbian Mayan city, it depicts a mythological scene with the Moon Goddess.

Cacoa was made into a drink originally, called *chocolatl* by the Aztecs. The Spanish conquistador Hernan Cortes described the drink as divine and said that a cup of it allowed a man to walk all day without food.

PART·ONE

RAW CHOCOLATE MAKING:

THEORY AND PHILOSOPHY

THEORY AND PHILOSOPHY BEHIND RAW CHOCOLATE

RAW CHOCOLATE: THE CULTURE

Did you know that there is an entire raw chocolate culture with its own set of values, ethics and principles?

A culture into which you are now about to enter.

As a part of that culture you will be sharing in the knowledge and wisdom of all of those who have so far contributed to it.

So, for example:

- o What is it that makes raw chocolate so special?
- o Why is raw chocolate thought of as a highly nourishing superfood?
- o Why make raw chocolate in preference to buying processed commercial chocolate?

So grab yourself a cup of hot chocolate, get comfortable, and let's begin with:

What Do I Mean by Raw Chocolate?

WHAT IS RAW CHOCOLATE?

(Or rather, WHAT DO *I* MEAN BY RAW CHOCOLATE?)

CAN CHOCOLATE BE RAW?

There have been debates within the raw food movement as to what exactly constitutes raw food and, in relation to raw chocolate, whether it is even possible, when the natural processing of the cacao is taken into account.

In particular, the temperatures reached when the beans are fermented.

LAWS FOR RAW?

There is no legislation at the time of writing that covers what is 'raw' but it's possible that will change in the future.

Rather than getting into the details of this debate here in this book, I will let you know what I mean by raw chocolate.

You can investigate it for yourself if you like, of course.

What I mean by raw chocolate is simple: I make chocolate using a gentle, low heat process. Wherever I can, I use cacao that is described as 'unroasted' or 'raw', so that it, too, has been treated gently and at a low heat.

Gentle, low-heat chocolate making

I always use organic cacao butter and powder. In fact, wherever possible all my ingredients are organic. This is part of the culture around raw chocolate and I'll talk more about that later on.

The chocolate I will be showing you how to make here will have one ingredient in it that isn't raw – the sweetener – either maple syrup or coconut sugar.

They are the best sweeteners that I have found, but some raw chocolatiers have experimented with raw sweeteners, and we'll be looking at some of these options later on in the book.

TEMPERING RAW CHOCOLATE

An important part of making good quality chocolate is tempering.

Tempering involves melting the ingredients. When I temper the chocolate I bring it up to around 42 degrees centigrade, which is widely considered as keeping within the window of what is raw.

Because it won't work under 42 degrees and because I am making chocolate using simple equipment, sometimes it goes over that heat. But I don't worry too much about it. The important thing is the gentle treatment.

For me, raw chocolate is chocolate that has been produced using minimal processing, as close to the natural food – cacao – as is possible *for me* to make. And that is what you will learn to do in this book.

Hand tempering is great to learn to do at home

WHAT ARE THE BENEFITS OF RAW CHOCOLATE?

IT'S ALL ABOUT THE CACAO

Why *raw* chocolate? Why make chocolate with unroasted cacao?

Raw chocolate always has high levels of cacao solids. Chocolate with high levels of cacao, (or cocoa), is the best chocolate treat we can eat. This is because the cacao bean, in its raw form, is full of nutrients.

The latin name is *theobroma cacao*. The theobroma part means 'food of the gods' from the Greek 'theos' – god and 'broma' – food.

The roasting and high levels of processing that most commercial chocolate undergoes affects these nutrients to some extent and those of us who are passionate about raw chocolate like to keep the nutrients as intact as possible.

As far as I am concerned, all good quality chocolate can be delicious but most of it is high in refined sugar, sometimes containing more sugar than chocolate itself.

GOOD FATS

You might also find commercial chocolate has cheaper non-chocolate fats and emulsifiers added, which doesn't happen with raw chocolate making. Raw chocolate makers always use high quantities of cacao butter, even though it is the most expensive ingredient in chocolate making.

Cacao butter is the highest ingredient in my chocolate – the chocolate I will be teaching you to make in this book.

Cacao butter is a very stable fat. It can stay fresh for two years or more. It is hard at room temperature. It has a melting point around that of our body's temperature which means it melts easily in the mouth and makes it very pleasant to use on our skin.

I believe that highly stable fats are good for us to eat – good for our skin, heart and brain.

I am not trained in this area, however, and there is conflicting advice between nutritionists, and governmental guidelines with regards to saturated fat.

If you are interested in this, there is plenty of information on the internet for you to get your teeth into.

Cacao butter chunks

Cacao butter

High-cacao chocolate

OTHER GOOD THINGS IN CACAO

The raw cacao bean has high levels of magnesium which helps us to deeply relax and also helps to build strong bones.

Maybe it's a co-incidence but when I fell and broke my wrist a few years ago and needed surgery on it, the surgeon said he found I had unexpectedly strong bones for a woman in her fifties.

It won't surprise you to hear that I regularly eat raw chocolate!

There are chemical constituents within cacao that are very similar to those our bodies make when we are excited, focussed or in love. Eating chocolate can give us similar feelings.

The higher the cacao percentage in the chocolate you are eating, the better.

Dark chocolate has very useful levels of antioxidants according to various scientific sources[2] and keeping it raw minimises heat-damage.

The two major ingredients in our chocolate making are the cacao butter and the cacao powder. The recipe we will use here is 75% cacao, 75% raw / unroasted chocolate.

Ixcacao, the Mayan Goddess of Chocolate

Ixcacao (or Ixkakaw) was known under alternative names to the Aztecs and other ancient peoples of Mesoamerica. Ixcacao translates simply as *cacao woman*. Unsurprisingly, she was associated with happiness, abundance and knowledge!

THE BEAUTY OF HOMEMADE, HANDMADE CHOCOLATE

Children love making chocolate!

In this book I will show you how to make chocolate using the most natural ingredients, and by that I mean closest to the plant itself, and without having to use machinery.

Handmade. Homemade. Close to nature.

When we make our own chocolate at home, we can customise it to our heart's content and to meet any special requirements of our family and friends.

This is one of the most enjoyable things for me: to be able to make bespoke chocolate so that people who would normally not be able to eat it can enjoy it.

REAL HANDMADE CHOCOLATE IS UNUSUAL

It's not common to make chocolate from scratch in the conventional chocolate world.

'Handmade chocolate' usually means the cook or chocolatier has used *couverture*: a type of chocolate with a relatively high amount of cocoa butter, which they melt down and use as they need to, including retempering it. They usually add their own flavours, inclusions and decorative touches.

This is a wonderful art, but it's not the same as making chocolate from scratch, by hand, which I will show you how to do in this book.

Raw chocolate is not widely available as couverture yet. This may change and then so will the raw chocolate culture. Using couverture means the chocolatier has a smoother chocolate to work with. Our chocolate will have a more grainy texture.

Couverture buttons

MORE CHOICES

If you make your own chocolate from scratch, you will be able to decide how to sweeten it and how much sweetener to put in it, and the ratio of cacao solids to other ingredients – in other words how *chocolaty* it is.

People's tastes vary and you might prefer a minimal amount of sweetener, especially as raw cacao doesn't have the common bitter taste that chocolate made from roasted beans can have.

Or you may have a sweet tooth and want to increase the amount of sweetener you use.

And, as I will show you, there are other ways you can sweeten your chocolate that you won't find in a couverture, like xylitol, erythritol, yacon, and powdered mulberries.

Some low-sugar options ~ yacon (top), mulberries and erythritol

NEAR AND FAR

I really enjoy bringing exotic foods into my home: like cacao from Peru and coconut sugar from Indonesia. Then I might add mint from my garden, or strawberries from a small-holding a few miles away. This is the way I like to mix it up and customise what I'm doing. Handmade and homemade can be such creative fun.

TRULY SATISFYING

In addition to this, it a really special undertaking when we make something by hand, especially chocolate which is usually machine-made.

Creating handmade chocolate connects you with something deep – that is personal to you – and those who you share your chocolate with will notice!

The more pleasure you take as you do it the better your chocolate will be!

Untempered chocolate making is a lovely thing to do with children

The pleasure of creating by hand

A handful of cacao nibs

CHILDREN WILL BENEFIT

How lovely for children to be able to see us creating something so delicious from scratch.

In a world of pretty much generic chocolate aimed at children, you will be giving those who see what you can do, and who may be even lucky enough to do it with you, the knowledge that chocolate can be delicious, healthy and **we** get to decide how it's created.

You might want to give a young child, who's never had chocolate before, a very low-sugar or unsweetened piece so that their delicate refined taste buds are awakened gently. They won't need much of course, because cacao is strong and can be stimulating.

It is truly a wonderful thing to do, to be able to make chocolate that is uniquely yours.

Made by your hands. In your home. A gift to yourself and the world.

THE RAW CHOCOLATE CULTURE

Raw chocolates made by world-renowned teacher, Amy Levin

A genre of food production and consumption having its own value system? What a curious idea! Well, the raw chocolate world has. There is nothing quite like it, in the food world.

Although the raw chocolate community is comprised of many individuals from all over the planet, with differing perspectives and priorities, I am proud that my chocolate creating has its roots in such a set of values.

So, what values and ethics might these be? You've probably got a very good idea already but it's so pleasing to me to recognise and acknowledge them here.

And as you embark upon your raw chocolate making, you are now entering this culture.

WHAT DOES IT LOOK LIKE?

Raw food is predominantly dairy-free and vegan, except with bee products being used occasionally.

The raw food movement sees plant food as being a prime form of nourishment for our bodies and of great benefit to the planet.

The same is true with organic production. The raw chocolate culture celebrates food that is produced organically or without agricultural chemicals.

I have never come across any raw chocolate business that doesn't do this.

Raw treats made by Amy Levin

LIVING FOOD

Treats that are full of vitality are what the raw chocolate culture consistently reaches for. Health-giving, nourishing sweets are prized highly.

So, we don't use refined sugar and much attention has been, and is, focussed on finding alternative sweeteners that are unrefined and even raw.

Raw sweet treats can be healthy and nourishing

FAIRNESS IN TRADE

Raw chocolate makers commonly source ethically produced products.

This is what Tree Harvest, who supply chocolate ingredients and who are based in Devon, UK, say about their cacao;

'Our Peruvian cacao is cultivated by small farmer co-operatives. The criollo variety is considered to be the king of cacao because it is the most ancient. It is not a hybrid and produces high quality beans of fine flavours and aromas, constituting an important percentage in the production of fine chocolate.

Minimum possible processing is used with this bean, applying low fermentation and low temperature without roasting, by means of unique methods to maintain its natural purity and quality.'

RAW CHOCOLATE INFLUENCERS:

AMY LEVIN / OOSHA

Amy Levin, raw chocolate pioneer

Amy Levin has been described as the world's leading raw chocolatier and pastry chef. She must also be the world's leading raw chocolate teacher. She has inspired thousands of people all over the world through her online and live courses. She is a very generous teacher, giving much of her material – recipes and mini courses - away for free. I have taken several of her fantastic raw chocolate online courses and would unreservedly recommend them.

One of the special things about Amy's recipes, which she regularly posts online, is how she likes to recreate nostalgia-filled sweets from her American childhood, using high quality natural ingredients.

This is what she says about her passion for chocolate,

'I never planned on it being my passion, but I don't think we can control these things. Passion creeps up on us and takes hold of us. It drives the boat and we just navigate it as best as we can. Working with chocolate allows me to express myself in a way I was never able to do through other forms of cooking. I think it's the emotional connection I have to sweets from being a child that really connected me so deeply.'

Raw chocolate by Amy Levin

PABLO SPAULL / FOREVER CACAO

Pablo Spaull of Forever Cacao

Pablo Spaull, from Forever Cacao in Wales, works with the Asháninka people in Peru. These cacao growers use no pesticides or chemical fertilisers and all follow organic farming methods.

Pablo uses their heirloom criollo beans in his chocolate and is part of a network of organisations that support these cacao producers so they can carry on their work.

The indigenous communities work together with this network to protect 2.5 million acres of pristine rainforest, safeguarding wild ancient cacao and other crops they rely on.

Pablo says,

'You could call this viral conservation, with village after village lining up to protect their forest.'

Pablo's mission is:

o To safeguard Asháninka heirloom cacao strains
o To buy direct and pay a higher price for quality
o To protect endangered Amazon rainforest
o To make the best tasting raw chocolate
o To eat chocolate every day (for the purposes of work, of course)

THE RAW FOOD CULTURE HAS CHANGED THE WAY FOOD IS PRODUCED

Raw chocolate and raw food have developed so much that a brand new area of food production has been created.

This is especially evident in the area of chocolate, cakes and other sweet treats, although delicious savouries are also produced, like breads, crackers, pizza bases and crisps which are fantastic alternatives to the cooked equivalent.

Raw cookies ready to go into the dehydrator

DEHYDRATION: A FOOD REVOLUTION

In the raw food world, dehydrators are used instead of ovens. They are invaluable to people who eat a raw food diet to a greater or lesser extent.

So what are the great things about using a dehydrator?

Vitamins and other nutrients that are heat-sensitive are better preserved.

By using a dehydrator you can create nutrient-rich foods such as activated and dehydrated nuts; 'buckwheaties'; raw sweet pie crusts; 'cheesecake' bases; raw crystalised ginger using the sweetener of your choice; orange, mint and other 'sugars' using erythritol or xylitol or maple syrup; and raw granola to name just a few.

Collecting rose petals from the garden, for dehydrating

You can dry your own garden products like strawberries, raspberries and cherries to put in your chocolate. I also like to use rose petals.

Garden-to-bar chocolate inclusions!

Rose petals used in chocolate

Dehydrators warm raw food – you can create warm biscuits or brownies, for example. There are multiple trays in a dehydrator so you can dry, melt or warm several different things at once.

You can dry foods at the temperature of a desert sunshine – almost sun-dried!

You can create natural food colours by dehydrating and powdering such things as beetroot, turmeric, carrot and spinach. The resulting powders can be used to colour your sweets.

I find a dehydrator an indispensible piece of kitchen kit. In fact, I have two. One I use for professional chocolate making purposes where hygiene is of great importance, and one I keep for drying wild herbs and seaweeds for my personal use.

Dehydrating candied nuts

Mayan glyph for cacao

LET'S COMPARE:
RAW CHOCOLATE WITH CONVENTIONAL CHOCOLATE

Bars of handmade raw chocolate

All chocolate can be delicious!

Having said that, in this section we're going to look at the features that raw chocolate has, compared to features of more conventionally produced chocolate.

PROCESSING

Raw chocolate makers use minimal **processing**. **Low heat** is used when making the chocolate, which to keep it raw is 45 degrees Celsius and below.

With conventional chocolate, there are high levels of **processing**. The cacao beans are roasted to around 150 or 160 degrees Celsius.

Raw chocolate is usually made by artisan producers in **small micro batches,** or handmade.

It will have a more **textured** grainy consistency unless a stone grinder is used.

Conventional chocolate can be both **factory made** and **artisan made**. It has a smooth **texture**. Long periods of grinding and *conching* are essential.

Unroasted cacao has a simple **flavour** profile. Complicated layers of **flavours** can be developed through the roasting processes used by conventional chocolate producers.

STANDARDS

Raw chocolate is almost always **organic** and the producers will source agrochemical-free ingredients. Within the conventional chocolate market **organic** chocolate is a niche.

SUGAR

The proportion of **sugar** to cacao is relatively low in raw chocolate. It can still be up to as much as a quarter but compared to conventional chocolate that is fairly low. No refined white cane sugar is used.

With conventional chocolate the proportion of **sugar** to cacao varies and can be much higher than raw chocolate, including being the first ingredient and as much as half of the bar actually being refined sugar. Refined white cane sugar is almost always the primary sugar used.

Conventional, mass-produced chocolate

SWEETENERS

A variety of **sweeteners** can be used when making raw chocolate, allowing for healthy options. Highly refined sweeteners are rarely used, except for **sugar alcohols** such as erythritol or xylitol and even they are still fairly unusual. They are really helpful for people who want zero sugar in their chocolate.

Conventional chocolate is more likely to use the sugar alcohol maltitol, as a zero sugar sweetener, and maltitol can cause digestive upset.

CACAO LEVELS

Raw chocolate is **cacao-dense**. As far as fats go, it's only ever made with cacao butter except for the occasional use of coconut oil but that cannot be used in tempered chocolate.

Raw chocolate has a lot of actual chocolate in it!

Conventional chocolate is sometimes mixed with cheaper **non-chocolate fat**, which means there's less cacao in it.

DAIRY

Raw chocolate is **dairy free** and **gluten free** by nature, by default.

It is almost always **vegan** although occasionally bee pollen and honey are used.

With conventional chocolate, **dairy free** and **gluten free** are niche markets.

Vegan is also a niche market.

Raw chocolate is dairy-free

NUTRIENTS

In raw chocolate, **nutrients** that are affected by heat remain stable.

With conventional chocolate, some **nutrients are lost** in the heating.

ADDITIVES

There are few, if any, additives to be found in raw chocolate. You are unlikely to find **soya** lecithin in it.

However, in conventional chocolate, emulsifiers and milk powders are often used as additives. **Soya** is also a common additive.

ENERGY LEVELS

Raw chocolate is often experienced anecdotally as deeply satisfying, uplifting, energising or relaxing.

Anecdotally, conventional chocolate is often experienced as creating sluggish, lethargic feelings in the body.

Although these lists aren't exhaustive, I've been able to give you a comparison of some of the main differences between raw and processed chocolate.

You can probably appreciate why I love to make my own raw chocolate. It is full of natural vital ingredients. People who try it soon come to appreciate just how wonderful raw chocolate is.

CACAO (OR COCOA) PERCENTAGE

WHAT DOES IT MEAN?

I'd like to say here that the words *cacao* and *cocoa* can be, and are, used interchangeably. I usually use cacao to mean the unroasted product and cocoa to mean roasted.

Cacao, or cocoa, percentage simply means how much of the chocolate is made from the products of the cacao bean.

So, if we make 100 g of chocolate and it contains:

- 50 g cacao butter
- 25 g cacao powder
- 25 g coconut sugar

it is then a **75% chocolate** or, put another way, it contains **75% cacao**.

In any good quality chocolate the remainder of the percentage will be what it's sweetened with.

Lesser quality chocolate will be made up of other ingredients as well as the sugar.

Any additions like nuts and fruit aren't taken into account – it's how much cacao the chocolate itself is made up of that matters.

The chocolate I teach you how to make here is 75%. The remaining 25% is the coconut sugar or maple syrup.

A high percentage of cacao doesn't always indicate a better chocolate but it often does.

It will certainly indicate that you are getting a lot of actual cacao or cocoa in your chocolate.

Ingredients for tempered raw chocolate ~ RATIO 2:1:1

OTHER SWEETENERS

Dried mulberries are deliciously sweet

My preferred way to sweeten untempered chocolate is to use maple syrup and I love using coconut sugar for tempered chocolate.

Let's now look at other sweeteners that you might want to use in your chocolate.

This will help you choose what works best for you and also give you a good overview of the sweeteners that are available.

This area of food is expanding all the time so there is sure to be even more to look forward to in the future.

For instance, I recently discovered organic sun-dried cane juice crystals. This product purports to be 'truly raw cane juice crystals'. The significance of this is that what is usually sold as 'raw cane sugar' simply means unrefined cane sugar, but will still have been heated to high temperatures. This new product has been dried in the sun, so any nutrients that are sensitive to heat will remain intact.

My initial experiments with this in tempered chocolate have been very promising and I like very much that there is always something new to discover.

NATURAL SWEETENERS OR ZERO-SUGAR SWEETENERS?

There are some products with zero-sugar content that have been refined, and there are some products with a low-sugar content that are whole foods but as yet I've not found a suitable one that's both zero-sugar and unrefined.

SUGAR ALCOHOLS: ZERO-SUGAR

First let's looks at what are known as sugar alcohols. They will be of particular interest to anyone on a low carb or ketogenic diet, a sugar-free diet or are making chocolate for someone with diabetes. They usually look just like white sugar, although you can get some caramel coloured. They don't contain any alcohol.

Erythritol

ERYTHRITOL

Erythritol is my preferred one in this group. It occurs naturally in some fruits and fermented foods but for commercial purposes is created from fermented sucrose.

It is nearly as sweet as sugar but has almost no calories. It doesn't affect blood sugar and it doesn't cause tooth decay.

Compared to other sugar alcohols such as xylitol, it's easier to digest. Personally, I experience erythritol as a benign, neutral, way of sweetening chocolate.

It is worth mentioning that **erythritol has a cooling effect in chocolate.** This is great alongside a mint flavour for instance, but not so good in something like a rum and raisin bar.

Being able to create zero-sugar chocolate if needed can be very valuable. You can use it as a straight weight-for-weight swop with coconut sugar.

I would always look for GM-free erythritol as sometimes it is produced using genetically modified corn, apparently.

When you use erythritol or any of the other sugar alcohols in chocolate making, powder it as you would the coconut sugar so you get as much smoothness as possible.

XYLITOL

Another sugar alcohol that's used in chocolate making is xylitol. Like erythritol, it looks very much like white sugar. Xylitol has more calories that erythritol but 40% less than ordinary sugar.

It occurs in our bodies and also in some fruits and vegetables. When it's manufactured it's often derived from birch bark.

Again, I'd recommend that you select non-GMO xylitol as it can also be made from genetically modified corn and sugar beet.

Like erythritol, it doesn't cause tooth decay and is often found in chewing gum and toothpastes. It has the same cooling effect as erythritol has.

Xylitol can cause bloating, apparently, but I've not experienced that. Everybody is different, of course.

Also, it's dangerous for dogs, but then, so is chocolate.

I've got mixed feelings about these products. I really appreciate having access to them but they aren't as natural as I'd like, so I'd say – do your own research, trust your body and its response to them.

NATURAL SWEETENERS: STEVIA

The stevia plant has sweet leaves!

Stevia is a South American plant that has leaves that taste really sweet. It is much, much sweeter than ordinary sugar. The leaf has a strange and distinctive taste.

You can buy organic stevia leaf powder. Experiment with it if zero sugar is important to you as it has no calories and it isn't experienced by our bodies as sugar. However, its distinctive taste will be present in the natural unrefined stevia leaf powder.

Because it's so sweet it isn't a straight swop – proportion wise – for the coconut sugar in these recipes, so the results won't be the same.

You can also buy stevia extracts in powder and liquid form and you could experiment with them, especially in untempered chocolate where liquids can be used. You should be able to find stevia extract products that don't have the distinctive after taste.

Check the labels as some stevia products also contain erythritol, which you might not want.

MULBERRIES

Mulberries are a lovely fruit and they can be dried, powdered and used as an unrefined, *whole food* sweetener in place of coconut sugar.

They are a really delicious way of sweetening and go beautifully in chocolate. Recipe-wise, use the same amount as coconut sugar.

Mulberries

LUCUMA

Lucuma is a Peruvian fruit that can be bought as a powder and used as a part replacement for the coconut sugar.

Lucuma fruit is dried and can be used to sweeten chocolate

Raw chocolate makers often use this if they want a lower-sugar chocolate.

And it's available raw.

It's got its own distinct flavour so check it out if you enjoy experimenting.

MESQUITE

Mesquite is another Peruvian food, which can be used in the same way as lucuma, as a part replacement for coconut sugar in the recipes in this book.

YACON

Yacon also comes from Peru. It's a root that comes in both powder and syrup form. It's got a very pleasant taste.

It's a favourite with those who want both low-sugar and whole foods, but to my taste, the powder isn't sweet enough.

I love to use the syrup, however, and recommend you try it for yourself.

Yacon comes in both syrup and powder form

MAPLE SUGAR

Maple sugar is another option which I imagine would be delicious.

I've not tried it yet!

Maple sugar

OTHER NATURAL SWEETENERS: LIQUIDS

When you're thinking about sweetening untempered chocolate you have more choices because you can use liquids. In addition to MAPLE SYRUP and YACON SYRUP, you can use:

AGAVE SYRUP

Agave has a mild flavour, especially light agave, and that might be a good choice if you want the sweetener to take a back seat. Some people avoid it because of its high-fructose content.

HONEY

Honey has lots going for it and is a fantastic choice if you want to make all-raw chocolate and can get hold of raw honey.

It's not suitable for vegans, of course.

TO SUM UP

These will all give you an idea of what options you have to sweeten your chocolate. There are lots of products out there to suit your particular preferences and requirements. I hope you enjoy experimenting as much as I do.

Liquid gold – honey is an option for non-vegans

Let's Make Chocolate

PART·TWO

RAW CHOCOLATE MAKING:

THE PRACTICE

EQUIPMENT AND TOOLS YOU'LL NEED

Now that you've read about how wonderful this type of chocolate is, you are probably raring to get started.

But we can't make raw chocolate without having the necessary equipment. So that's what we will be looking at next.

Read this section at least a few days before you begin your chocolate making in case there is anything you need to buy. The great thing about raw chocolate making is that you don't need a load of specialised equipment, at least in the beginning. And in many cases, you'll already have it in your kitchen.

MOULDS

A selection of polycarbonate and silicone moulds

To be able to make chocolate you will need moulds into which the melted chocolate can be poured. As the chocolate solidifies, it then takes on the shape of the mould.

As you might have guessed, moulds are really fun, because you can use them to give your chocolate any shape you want - hearts, flowers, animals, letter, bars - if you can imagine it there will probably be a mould for it!

There are also moulds that enable you to create beautiful patterns on your chocolate. I love these because they make the final product look really professional.

However, when you're starting out you don't need to have specialised chocolate moulds. If you wanted you could even use an ice cube tray. When I started out I used anything I could find.

SILICONE MOULDS

As you're going to begin your learning with untempered chocolate, you will need one or more silicone moulds. These are great. They're cheap so you can buy lots of different ones if you like and really have fun.

Silicone moulds come in a great variety of shapes and sizes

They are perfect for when you're starting out. They have the advantage that untempered chocolate can be pushed out of them because they are flexible.

They can be bought online or in your local kitchen supplies shop.

POLYCARBONATE MOULDS

Professional chocolatiers tend to use polycarbonate moulds.

The results can be beautiful if you use professional moulds. If you want to sell your chocolate or present it to impress, this is what you will want to buy.

Polycarbonate mould

Although they are more expensive than silicone moulds, I have obtained some second hand ones at a very reasonable price and the results are perfect.

However, if second hand polycarbonate moulds have not been looked after well, the final chocolate product may not look so good.

Polycarbonate moulds need to be polished before use and treated gently. Wash them by hand in warm soapy water.

Untempered chocolate won't come out of these moulds so they are for tempered chocolate only.

BOWLS

You'll need to have a set of bowls. I recommend stainless steel as they are much easier for tempering.

They are lightweight which is important because you will be holding the bowl in the air with one hand!

And they don't retain the heat like glass or ceramic, at a point when you will need to cool your melted chocolate promptly. You will need a minimum of two 4 litre bowls but it's handy to have the extra large one to help cool the melted chocolate quickly.

I also have two small 2 litre bowls which are great for keeping measured ingredients at the ready.

Those don't need to be stainless steel, however.

Whatever you have in your cupboards will be fine.

I use one large 5 litre bowl and one 4 litre bowl, like these.....

Stainless steel bowls

THERMOMETERS

When making chocolate, and particularly raw chocolate, temperature is always a crucial consideration.

Because of this you are going to need a food thermometer when you start out.

Later on, with experience, you'll be able to gauge when your chocolate is in temper.

A thermometer makes this so easy, however.

I use an infrared thermometer and a corded digital one.

I recommend you get one with a nice easy-to-read screen.

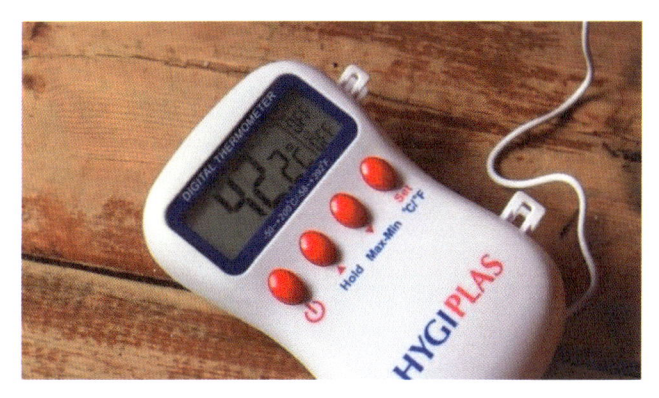

Corded digital thermometer

GRINDING YOUR SUGARS

A coffee bean or spice grinder is an important piece of equipment.

You will be using it to powder your sweeteners before you melt your ingredients together. Make sure it's not been used for strong spices that might taint your chocolate.

However, personally I wouldn't be concerned about a lingering coffee taste as chocolate and coffee are very compatible.

You will need a coffee grinder

BAIN-MARIE

You will need a bain-marie set up. This is also known as a double boiler. This means a saucepan with a small amount of water in the bottom, upon which you put your large stainless steel bowl containing your ingredients.

Make sure the water in the pan won't touch the bottom of the bowl and overheat the chocolate.

The pan needs a lid so that you can contain the steam when you heat the water, before you put the bowl on top of the pan.

You don't want a kitchen filled with steam because moisture and tempered chocolate don't mix!

Double boiler or bain-marie

DEHYDRATOR

A dehydrator will be really useful, if not essential. I have the professional level Excalibur dehydrator and I would highly recommend it. It is expensive, however, at between £160 and £400 or about $200 to $500, depending on size.

The Excalibur dehydrator is well worth investing in

There are much cheaper ones like this at £40, which would be fine to begin with.

The less expensive Callow dehydrator

You could even use your oven, on a really low heat, although you might not be able to keep the temperature at the level of what is considered 'raw'.

If this is not paramount to you and you are just starting out, using a low oven is fine as you learn.

OTHER EQUIPMENT

Dedicate a chopping board especially for your chocolate making, to avoid the chocolate picking up strong flavours from other food.

You will use it for chopping cacao butter or nuts and other ingredients.

Even this is not essential in the beginning as cacao butter is now available in the form of buttons that don't need chopping but it's a nice thing to have for your creations.

You'll need a good, sharp knife. Again, dedicate one to your chocolate making if possible.

I like this 10 inch cook's knife.

A knife dedicated to chocolate is nice to have

You will need a sieve. You probably already have one.

You'll need some kitchen scales, you've probably got some of those, too. I use digital ones.

You'll also require a silicone spatula. It will be used for stirring and for clearing the chocolate from one bowl to another during the tempering process.

You'll also need a tablespoon or two. I have a couple dedicated to chocolate but any from your kitchen drawer will do.

You may also wish to have some food gloves so that when you handle the chocolate you don't get finger prints on, especially if they are for gifts or to sell.

For storing your chocolate, gather some airtight containers and have some greaseproof paper to protect your creations.

EQUIPMENT CHECKLIST

- Moulds
- Polishing cloth for polycarbonate moulds
- Bowls
- Thermometer
- Coffee grinder
- Bain-marie set up
- Dehydrator
- Sieve
- Scales
- Spatula
- Chopping board
- Knife
- Tablespoons
- Airtight food containers
- Greaseproof paper
- Gloves (optional)

INGREDIENTS

Now that you know what equipment you will be using to make your chocolate, let's take a look at what ingredients you will need to begin.

CACAO

Of course your main ingredient will be cacao, also known as cocoa.

Cacao is a beautiful food to be working with. These are fresh cacao pods. What amazing colours!

Inside the pods is the fruit. This consists of a light-coloured pulp, within which are the seeds or cacao beans.

Right – vibrantly coloured cacao pods

Inside a cacao pod

Cacao fruit

I've heard the pulp is delicious, likened to the taste of lemonade. It can be brewed into an alcoholic beverage.

CACAO TREES

Cacao trees grow near to the equator. They're quite small (growing to about 4 to 8 meters in height) and in their natural habitat grow under a canopy of bigger trees which protect them from direct sun and wind, which they don't like.

According to the Fairtrade Foundation, 90% of the world's cacao growing is done on small family farms.

Traditional farms plant the trees in the shade and amongst other crops.

An early illustration of cacao beans drying, and a cacao tree flourishing in the shade of a taller tree

It seems that on large plantations the cacao trees don't have the benefit of the protective canopy and the diverse crops, and so need more human intervention to keep them strong and pest free.

CACAO PROCESSESSING

Cacao beans after fermenting and drying

The **cacao beans** are dried and fermented. They are then processed, which turns them into **cacao paste**.

The paste can come in chunks or buttons.

It can also be referred to as **cacao liquor** or **cacao mass**.

Cacao paste chunks

The paste is further processed to separate it into **cacao butter** and **cacao powder**: roughly half and half. **Cacao powder** will look familiar to you. It looks just like cocoa powder.

Cacao and cocoa powder look the same

Which it is, really. Except that, for use in raw chocolate, it's not made from roasted beans.

Hot chocolate – a very good use for cacao powder!

Cacao butter can come in chunks or in buttons.

SOURCING THE BEST

We will be using the finest ingredients for our chocolate making.

I usually work with Peruvian cacao butter and cacao powder. It is minimally processed, described as raw or unroasted, or virgin. It is always organic.

There are three types of cacao bean, *criollo* being the finest. Look out for that.

I often buy my cacao products from Amazon. In the UK, I would also recommend Tree Harvest who are based in Devon and Indigo Herbs, based in Glastonbury. Both have great customer service, friendly and personal. And you can buy Indigo Herbs products through Amazon.

COCONUT SUGAR

Chocolate, as most of us like it, needs to be sweetened. There's lots of fun to be had here!

My favourite sweetener for making tempered chocolate is coconut sugar. It's also known as coconut palm sugar or – coconut blossom sugar. What an evocative name!

It doesn't taste of coconut at all. Instead, it has a lovely rich caramel taste and a warm-biscuity aroma, both of which complement chocolate beautifully.

Coconut sugar complements raw chocolate beautifully

It is made by extracting the sap from the stems of coconut palm flowers, using quite simple methods.

Coconut palm

The sap is then heated to evaporate the water content, leaving the crystalised sugar.

So it's not a raw product.

I like coconut sugar because it is a whole food – in other words only water is taken out and nothing else is added – and because the processing involved is simple and minimal.

MAPLE SYRUP

My favourite sweetener for making untempered chocolate, where we can use liquids, is maple syrup. In fact, maple syrup is my favourite sweet thing ever. There really is nothing like it.

It contains numerous antioxidants, as well as important minerals and vitamins.

In fact, indigenous communities in Canada have used maple syrup to ward off infections for a very long time.

What a wonderful gift from the beautiful maple tree!

Maple syrup

SALT

Now, salt and chocolate is such a mouth watering combination! I always put a pinch of salt in the chocolate I am making.

I have a great love and respect for quality salt. I use it in all sorts of ways, not only in food.

It adds a certain special something to the chocolate. It makes sugar taste sweeter – now that's amazing, isn't it? It has a magical way of bringing out all of the fabulous flavours in the chocolate and I've also read that it modifies bitter tastes.

My preferred salt is pink Himalayan crystal salt and a pinch or two has gone in my chocolate every time for years.

Of course, you can play around with whatever salt appeals to you. Maybe a local sea salt or one from a far away place?

Salt field work in Vietnam

HERE'S WHAT YOU'LL NEED

This is what you'll need for 100g of chocolate and the proportions are really simple so you'll be able to easily increase or decrease your batch if you need to.

Ingredients for 100g Raw Chocolate

- 50 g raw, unroasted, or cold-pressed organic cacao butter
- 25 g raw or unroasted, organic cacao powder
- 25 g coconut sugar OR 25 g maple syrup
- A pinch of your favourite salt
- For the first batch we will be using food-grade, organic peppermint essential oil

You can buy your ingredients in bulk if you like because all these products keep well in a temperate climate although it is better to keep essential oils in the fridge or in a cool place.

Keep your bags sealed and make sure your cacao powder and coconut sugar are kept dry.

I fold my bags over at the top once I've opened them, reseal them and peg them closed.

Or you might want to keep them in kitchen containers.

Containers for your chocolate ingredients

I use a peg to keep my bags closed

RAW CHOCOLATE (100g)
50g Cacao butter
25g Cacao powder
25g Coconut sugar OR
25g Maple syrup
Pinch Pink Himalayan salt

PREPARING YOUR CHOCOLATE MAKING SPACE

We've looked at the equipment you'll need as well as the ingredients you'll be using. Now I'll show you how I prepare for a chocolate making session.

I've been making raw chocolate for a number of years now, and I've realised that the secret of making great chocolate is how you feel as you're doing it.

The better *I feel* when I begin and as I work, the better my chocolate turns out.

When you start a chocolate making session, it's really worth taking the time to create a beneficial environment for yourself to work in. The more organised and orderly it is, the smoother and more enjoyable your experience will be. Then you'll be able to easily slip into the chocolate making zone!

As I've said before, allow yourself plenty of time for a session.

Two hours if it's your first time, or even longer.

Prepare your surfaces, making sure everything is dry. You don't want any moisture getting into your chocolate, especially if you're going to temper it.

The clearing away of unnecessary kitchen items and the cleaning of the space you'll be using can be a great transition between doing whatever it was you were doing before and beginning your chocolate session.

I see this time as a chance to get into a more mindful state and to focus on what I'm about to do.

Almost like a pre-session ritual.

In my household, when I'm making chocolate everyone knows I'm not to be disturbed! I don't answer the door and no one else uses the kitchen. I love getting totally absorbed in what I am doing.

That's when the creative ideas flow!

Of course, you might want to make chocolate with other people and it's great to do that with untempered chocolate.

However, even now, I need to concentrate when I am tempering and give the chocolate my full attention.

Chocolate making with others can be a lovely thing to do

All equipment and utensils need to be completely dry.

If you have a dehydrator, you can pop your spoons, spatulas, chopping board and moulds in for five minutes or so to make sure.

The moulds will need to be taken out and at room temperature before you use them, however.

Extremes of temperature and sudden changes in temperature, aren't good for chocolate.

It's a good idea to always have spare batteries to hand, for your scales and your thermometer.

Get a couple of clean tea towels out or have the kitchen roll handy.

Gather together all the equipment you will be needing. You can refer back to the list on page 47.

Bain-marie, or double boiler

Prepare some space in the fridge, away from strong smells like onions, garlic and spices.

(You could leave your chocolate to set in a cool room and this will minimise any chance of tempered chocolate being affected by moisture but it will, of course, take a lot longer to set.)

Polycarbonate moulds need polishing before use

Give polycarbonate moulds a good polish with the cloth before you start. Cotton wool can also be used.

Prepare your bain-marie, or double boiler.

Get a large pan. Put a small amount of water in the bottom. You don't want the water to touch the bottom of the bowl but you need enough so there's no chance of it boiling dry.

Have a lid handy.

You can use a fridge to set your chocolate

That's your chocolate space set up nicely!

Checklist for prepping kitchen space before chocolate making session

* Clear, clean and dry kitchen surfaces
* Gather equipment together
* Polish any polycarbonate moulds
* Gather ingredients together

PREPARING YOUR INGREDIENTS

As part of preparing to make raw chocolate there are a couple of things you will need to do once you've set up your kitchen space and before you get going.

PREPARING CACAO BUTTER

The first is shaving the cacao butter. This is only necessary if you have butter that is in chunks rather than buttons.

The buttons melt easily and evenly.

If you have chunks they will need to be reduced to smaller even-sized pieces.

Cacao butter buttons don't need any preparation

You can weigh out what you need or shave it all, ready for future batches.

Put your chopping board on a tea towel to keep things steady.

Take a chunk of cacao butter and a large sharp knife.

Cacao butter chunks need to be prepared before use

Press down with your hand, keeping the chunk steady with the base of your hand.

Chop the pieces smaller and evenly.

Working with cacao butter leaves the skin on your fingers lovely and soft.

Cacao butter is a lovely ingredient to work with by hand

PREPARING COCONUT SUGAR

If you are going to temper your chocolate as I will show you how to do soon, you will need to powder your coconut sugar.

Coconut sugar

Most chocolate manufacturers use machines that grind the cacao-sugar mixture for long periods of time and that creates the smoothness many people are used to.

When coconut sugar arrives it is granulated and it doesn't blend well into the chocolate especially at the low temperatures we are using.

Even when powdered, the coconut sugar doesn't dissolve completely at low temperature so our handmade chocolate has more of a texture than machine-made chocolate.

We can enhance this characteristic by adding crunchy and chewy inclusions to the chocolate.

Once you have my prime recipe under your belt, you can add anything you want to create wonderful textures.

That being said, the pure simple chocolate bar is a delight in itself.

Tempered raw chocolate has texture

Powdering coconut sugar

To powder your coconut sugar we will be using a coffee, or spice grinder.

Weigh out what you will need, put it in the grinder and whizz it up for a few seconds.

You may need to do it in a couple of goes depending how much chocolate you are making.

The grinder doesn't hold very much at once.

Next weigh out the rest of your ingredients if you haven't already done so. Put the cacao butter into your large bowl, the cacao powder in a smaller bowl.

Put your powdered coconut sugar in another small bowl or if you are making simple untempered chocolate put your maple syrup in a suitable container. And don't forget your salt.

Now you're set up and all ready to make your first batch of raw chocolate!

All set up and ready to go!

THE MONEY THAT GROWS ON TREES

Cacao beans were considered so valuable that they were used as currency in ancient Central America. Montezuma, the emperor of the Aztec empire, paid his military and other workers in cacao beans. They continued to be used as currency in Mexico until 1887!

SIMPLE RAW (UNTEMPERED) CHOCOLATE

Let's get started and make our first batch of raw chocolate.

This is a recipe for 100g chocolate but the proportions are so simple you can increase or decrease as you wish.

I will be using *organic peppermint essential oil* to flavour the chocolate. Of course you can keep it simple and plain, especially for your first go.

INGREDIENTS

- 50 grams cacao butter, shaved or in buttons
- 25 grams cacao powder
- 25 grams maple syrup
- A pinch of your favourite salt
- Peppermint essential oil, if using for flavour

To make the untempered chocolate, we start with cacao butter.

And to that we add cacao powder, sieved, on top.

And a pinch of pink Himalayan crystal salt.

Then we add our gorgeous maple syrup ~ the same amount of maple syrup as cacao powder, which together makes the same amount as the cacao butter.

Let the cacao butter melt partially first before you stir it. This helps incorporate the powder.

Then stir now and again until it's melted completely.

If it's important to you that temperatures stay raw then you need to keep your food thermometer handy so that you don't heat your chocolate above 45 degrees Celsius, by accident.

Maple syrup is a perfect sweetener for untempered chocolate

Allow the cacao butter to melt somewhat before stirring

Bring a small amount of water to the boil. Make sure the water won't touch the bottom of your bowl, nor risk boiling dry.

Turn off the heat and put your bowl of ingredients on top of the pan.

When it's all melted you will have lovely, smooth liquid chocolate. Next, add peppermint essential oil to the chocolate, if you wish. I use food grade, organic peppermint from NHR Oils. You don't need very much, about five drops.

There will now be a gorgeous smell to enjoy! Mix the oil in. Have a little taste to make sure it's the right amount of peppermint. Mmm, warm liquid chocolate that's beautifully minty.

Take your melted chocolate. Use a suitable size spoon to fill the silicone mould of your choice.

Leave it to set a bit before you move it to the fridge because as it is so runny, it may spill and go over the edges of the mould. Alternatively, you can use a tray or board under the mould so it can go straight in the fridge.

Filling your mould on a board minimises drips when you move it

Remove from the fridge after 30 minutes or when the chocolate is set.

Chocolate comes out easily from silicone moulds

Carefully take out from the moulds. Untempered chocolate melts easily, so you will need to work quickly.

If my hands feel warm, I run them under cold water and dry them, before I begin.

You can use a sharp knife to trim any overflow. Make sure the chocolate is cold so it doesn't melt while you're handling it.

Trim any overflow chocolate

Here they are, looking delicious and ready to eat.

Untempered chocolate, fresh out of the moulds

Store untempered chocolate in the fridge, or even in the freezer.

Now you've made this first batch, I'd really like you to make lots of untempered chocolate and experiment with it. It's an easy and very delicious way to develop your relationship with chocolate. Then when you get onto making tempered chocolate you'll really notice the difference and you'll understand how beneficial it is to go onto the next stage of mastery!

Mint Chocolate Buttons

You can keep your untempered chocolate pure or enhance it with essential oils and a variety of other additions.

So, for your next batch, how about creating orange chocolate, with the sweet orange peel inclusions I'm going to show you next?

Cacao and Magnesium

In nature, one of the primary sources of magnesium is cacao.

Magnesium powers and supports the heart, the brain and the bones.

Magnesium relaxes muscles and increases flexibility.

Magnesium is the most deficient major mineral for those eating the average Western diet. Over 80% of Americans don't get enough.

Let's eat more chocolate!

CANDIED INCLUSIONS:

#1 MAPLE-CANDIED ORANGE PEEL

Next I'm going to show you how to candy orange peel with maple syrup and coconut sugar. It is an absolutely delicious combination and the little pieces that you'll end up with are fantastic in chocolate, of course.

This is what you'll need, based on four or five oranges, although you might want to make more as it's so good.

It keeps well in a jar or other container, so long as it's airtight.

MAPLE-CANDIED ORANGE INCLUSIONS

- 4 or 5 large organic oranges
- Half the weight of the orange peel of maple syrup
- The same again of coconut sugar
- A pinch of pink Himalayan salt or whatever your favourite salt is

Use organic oranges. Take a sharp knife and carefully slice the peel off. You can do it in small pieces or in long slithers. It doesn't matter. Even sizes is what you are aiming for.

Take your time. Don't rush. It is a lovely thing to do as your kitchen gets more and more aromatic with this gorgeous fruity smell.

You can use a microplane instead of a knife.

A microplane is another option

Citrus peel is really nutritious and we don't usually eat it so this is a fantastic way of getting the flavonoid-rich peel into our diet. For the next stage you'll need a bowl and spoon, as well as the prepared orange peel, the coconut sugar, maple syrup and a bit of salt.

Add all the ingredients together.

Mix all the ingredients together well

Give it a good mix so that the maple syrup, coconut sugar and salt can adhere nicely to the orange pieces.

It gives off such a warm summery smell!

Spread out the mixture onto a dehydrator Teflex sheet.

Spread it out thinly - about a single layer of orange peel.

This now goes into the dehydrator for twelve hours or more, depending on how it dries and also what time of day or night it is.

After that, flip the orange peel off the Teflex sheet onto the dehydrator mesh.

You might want to put a Teflex sheet or some greaseproof paper underneath the mesh because if the mixture is still quite wet, the syrup will run onto your table. And of course you don't want to lose any!

Dry further for another twelve hours or so, depending on the size of your orange pieces.

The picture above was taken after about twenty hours later. I could have taken it out sooner but it was night-time! That's the wonderful thing about using a dehydrator. It's slow food that you're preparing and you're very unlikely to overdo it.

If you want your candied orange pieces chewy, take them out sooner. They have good keeping qualities, especially when dried to the point when they are crisp.

But they are so delicious, (they taste like maple marmalade) that may not be relevant!

You can, of course, use them in any way you wish, including eating them as they are. But if you want to add them to chocolate, cut them or break them up into smaller pieces.

Adding a few drops of orange essential oil to your melted chocolate is a nice touch.

USING AN OVEN

If you don't have a dehydrator you can make this in your oven on its lowest setting, using a baking tray. Check it every hour or so and give the mixture a stir so that it dries out evenly. Depending on how small you cut the pieces and how low your oven is, it may take several hours. The results are different to a dehydrated version but still delicious.

Ingredients for Maple-Candied Orange Peel

ORANGE CHOCOLATES

Let's make some chocolates with this gorgeous Maple-Candied Orange Peel. You'll need:

INGREDIENTS

- 50 g shaved cacao butter, or buttons
- 25 g cacao powder
- 25 g maple syrup
- Few drops of food-grade organic orange oil
- Pinch of salt
- Maple Candied Orange Peel

You can change the amounts to suit yourself so long as you use the same proportions.

Using the untempered chocolate method that you've already learnt, sieve the cacao powder on top of the cacao butter. Add a pinch of salt to balance the sweetness. Add the maple syrup. And then add some organic sweet orange oil. Use about five drops, or to taste.

Put the bowl of ingredients on top of a bain-marie or double boiler, where there's a small amount of hot water in the bottom of the pan.

Make sure the bottom of the bowl doesn't touch the water.

It's a good idea to let the cacao butter melt a little before you stir the mixture. Keep an eye on the temperature because it can heat up very quickly, especially with small batches.

Chocolate can burn at 50 degrees or higher and then it's not much use.

Your melted chocolate will smell really lovely – warm and orangey!

Spoon it into silicone moulds. Add small pieces of Maple-Candied Orange Peel to each cavity. You might like to save a few for decoration. If you do, add them once the chocolate has begun to set a little.

Adding Maple-Candied Orange Peel to butterfly chocolates

Pop your moulds into the fridge for about thirty minutes, or until set. You could also put them in the freezer if you want to eat the chocolates really quickly!

Being able to use the freezer is one of the advantages of making untempered chocolate – with tempered chocolate we need to keep it away from moisture as much as possible so we wouldn't put it in the freezer.

Once the chocolates are set, carefully and promptly remove them from the moulds.

Now they're ready to enjoy!

Keep making lots of untempered chocolate in preparation for going onto learning tempering skills.

Making lots of untempered chocolate will really help your progress!

SO FAR...

In this book you have experimented with the wonderful pure and natural ingredients available for us to use.

You've learnt how enjoyable it can be to make handmade chocolate. Now you have at your very fingertips a great variety of ways of treating yourself and your loved ones to delicious healthy chocolate.

HOT CHOCOLATE DRINKING KEEPS KUNA INDIANS SUPER HEALTHY

The Kuna Indians of Panama are much healthier than their neighbours and live longer. They have extremely low levels of the most common killer diseases. Interestingly, they can drink up to forty cups of natural cocoa a week. It is believed that the high levels of flavonols and the chemical, epicatechin, in natural cocoa account for their supreme health[2].

TEMPERED RAW CHOCOLATE

Learning how to temper will enable you to make impressive chocolate and even go on to create a chocolate business of your own, if that's what you'd like to do.

The standards are high in the professional chocolate arena and raw chocolate standards are getting higher all the time, thanks to raw chocolate teachers like Amy Levin, who has been my inspiration.

WHAT IS TEMPERING AND WHY IS IT AMAZING TO LEARN?

Tempering is a craft, a science and an art, all rolled into one. You may be inspired to practice and practice the craft of tempering which will increase your ability to create impressive chocolate.

You can go deeply into the science, if that draws you. The science behind tempering is fascinating and learning about it will help you understand more about the nature of chocolate.

You can acquire the feel of the art of tempering, becoming tuned to its almost alchemical process.

WHAT IS TEMPERING?

Tempering is the precisely controlled heating, and cooling, of molten chocolate to correctly crystalise the cocoa butter within.

Tempered raw chocolate

This produces the required consistency and a smooth, glossy finish.

When liquid chocolate cools and re-solidifies, the fats start to crystalise. If this occurs in an uncontrolled fashion, a jumble of crystals, of varying sizes and types, form, causing the surface of the chocolate to appear mottled, streaky and dull. This makes the chocolate crumble rather than snap, when broken.

Chocolate is either tempered or untempered but within that, chocolate can be well-tempered or not so well-tempered. As your skills develop, you will learn about the fine nuances of what makes really well-tempered chocolate. After many years, I am still learning.

LET'S CONSIDER THE BENEFITS OF TEMPERING

BETTER LOOKING CHOCOLATE

If you learn how to temper you will be able to create better looking chocolate. Chocolate can have six different crystalline formations and there is one in particular that makes the final product look lovely and shiny and that's the one we're aiming for when we temper.

BETTER QUALITY CHOCOLATE

Tempered chocolate is considered to be better quality. It prevents what is called blooming: a whitish film, streaks or spots of cacao butter that form on the chocolate that doesn't look good even though it can still be eaten.

IT MEETS PROFESSIONAL STANDARDS

If you like the idea of going into business making healthy chocolate for others, tempering enables you to become a professional.

GOOD KEEPING QUALITIES

Tempered chocolate has a shelf life of months, even a year. It stays stable and good for that long.

Well-tempered chocolate won't change its appearance if it's kept in the right conditions, which are basically dry and cool.

It doesn't need to be kept in the fridge and shouldn't be, in fact. It won't melt at the lower temperatures that untempered chocolate will.

BETTER CONSISTENCY

Tempered chocolate will have a better consistency and what is called *mouth feel*. This is because the cacao butter fat is evenly distributed throughout so it's creamy without being fatty.

Tempered chocolate is hard and has a snap to it - which is what people expect when they bite into chocolate.

PROFESSIONAL MOULDS

You'll be able to use beautiful professional-looking moulds, like these, above.

Tempered chocolate contracts, making it possible for it to come out of the mould.

LAST BUT NOT LEAST

Finally, it's fun to learn something new about this food – chocolate- that you love.

There is a great sense of satisfaction that comes after your first tempered batch – I speak from my own experience. Especially if you've been making untempered bars - you'll be really ready for tempering and you'll love every minute of it.

HOW TO TEMPER RAW CHOCOLATE

Let's begin our tempering session!

I'll assume you've already prepared your chocolate-making space. Have a check back at the list of equipment you will need to hand.

Now prepare your ingredients (as you learnt to do in the earlier section), particularly cacao butter if yours is in chunks. Powder your coconut sugar and weigh out your ingredients.

This is what you'll need to make 100g chocolate.

INGREDIENTS

- 50 g cacao butter, shaved or in buttons
- 25 g cacao powder
- 25 g powdered coconut sugar
- Pinch of pink Himalayan salt

Put the cacao butter in your large stainless steel bowl. Sieve the cacao powder on top. Sieve the coconut sugar on top of that and add a pinch of salt.

Place the bowl of ingredients on top of a pan that has a small amount of hot water in it (bain-marie or double boiler). You don't want it to be actually boiling or simmering, as this will overheat the chocolate.

Let the cacao butter melt a little before you stir the mixture

After a couple of minutes, as the butter begins to melt, give the mixture a stir. It will vary how quickly it heats up, depending on the size of your batch.

When you're starting out, **you need to be alert at this stage.** Don't let it get too hot. It's easily done with small batches like this.

Take the temperature of your chocolate regularly

You will have more control over the temperature if you go on to make larger batches. Stirring it will even out the temperature.

Let the chocolate melt gently. Use your thermometer to keep an eye on the temperature. It needs to reach 42 degrees Celsius. You don't want it to go much higher than that, but you want all the cacao butter to melt.

When your melted chocolate is around 42 degrees, remove from the bain-marie and wipe the moisture from the underneath of your bowl.

Take it to your other stainless steel bowl and transfer the chocolate from one bowl to another, stirring in between. Lift the bowl up as you pour, to help it cool promptly.

Cooling from bowl to bowl helps the tempering process

Take advantage of the cool areas in the new bowl that haven't warmed up yet because that will help the chocolate cool down quickly.

Take the temperature as you're doing this and you'll see that in a small batch such as this, it will go down to 31.5 degrees quite quickly. You won't need to transfer it many times. In a larger batch, it will take longer.

Take the temperature of your melted chocolate in a pooled area, rather than in a thin area, as it will be at its warmest in those areas, of course. Keep mixing so that the temperature of the chocolate goes down evenly throughout.

When it's reached the desired temperature, you can fill your mould with the melted chocolate.

Polycarbonate mould being filled with tempered chocolate

Put into the fridge for about 15 minutes to cool.

After that, bring the mould out to reach room temperature, before you remove the chocolate.

In a polycarbonate mould, as tempered chocolate shrinks, it separates from the mould which makes it so much easier to come out.

Take a look at the bottom of the mould.

What you want is for it to be a silvery-grey colour, rather than a dark brown.

That means the chocolate is shrinking away from the mould underneath and is ready to come out.

These chocolates aren't ready yet

A silvery colour underneath is what you're looking for

Give the mould a gentle twist and the chocolate should come out easily.

You can give them a little tap against the table and allow them to fall on a soft surface such as a tea towel.

A tea towel protects your chocolates when you release them from the mould

Sometimes they don't all come out.

If that happens pop them back in the fridge for a little while.

(If they still don't come out, check the Chocolate Trouble chapter for troubleshooting help.)

Now your tempered chocolate is ready to eat!

If you aren't ready to eat it all straight away, it will keep very well.

Keep it in a dry, cool place, away from strong smells. Wrap in parchment or greaseproof paper and, as always, keep it in an airtight container.

THE TEMPERING PROCESS: RECAP

There are various methods of tempering, all basically intending to bring the chocolate to its best crystalline formation.

This is a recap of the method I teach here:

- Bring the chocolate gently up to 42 degrees. Below 42 degrees and the butter won't melt properly, above 42 and the chocolate moves away from what is considered 'raw'.

- Don't worry if it goes above this **by accident**, especially when you're learning, so long as it doesn't go too high - it will burn around 50 degrees and above.

- Bring it down to 31.5, keeping the chocolate moving. Transferring from one bowl to another is a great way of cooling it down quickly.

- It needs to go below 33 degrees for it to be tempered – we work with it at 31.5.

- Don't worry if it goes below 31.5, but as it cools down it will thicken and get harder to work with.

- If this does happen and you need to heat your chocolate up again, do it really carefully.

- If it goes past 33 degrees, you will need to retemper it, in other words take it right up to 42 again and bring it back down to 31.5.

- But that's not the end of the world because retempering chocolate can create a better final chocolate.

CONGRATULATIONS AND WELL DONE!

You now know how to temper raw chocolate.

This is fantastic because all sorts of opportunities are now open for you to use your chocolate in a variety of new ways.

You can create chocolate that is stable, has a good shelf life, and keeps its lovely appearance longer.

You can use your tempered chocolate to cover, or enrobe, truffles and other sweet treats.

You will be able to experiment with polycarbonate moulds that give really beautiful results.

I hope you are inspired to practice your tempering skills, and keep playing, remembering that it is an art that will improve over time as you get the feel of it.

By practising you will develop your hand-made chocolate craft.

And by practising you will also acquire more knowledge of tempering and chocolate in general, especially if a batch doesn't turn out as you were expecting and you are inspired to investigate more deeply the science of tempering.

How satisfying it is when you try it again and it works out well.

SCIENTISTS CALL CHOCOLATE A 'SUPERFOOD'

In a study sponsored by Hershey Chocolate[3], it was found that cocoa has significantly higher antioxidant levels than blueberries and other 'super fruits', so much so that they concluded that natural cocoa and dark chocolate warranted being called a *superfood.*

CANDIED INCLUSIONS:

#2 COCONUT CRISPIES

Now that you can make tempered chocolate, I'd like to show you one of my favourite things to do with it. Chocolate partnered with Candied Coconut Crispies is absolutely delicious.

We will be dehydrating the coconut mixture. However, you can use your oven on the lowest setting, if you wish. Like the Maple Candied Orange Peel, the Coconut Crispies will turn out different to the ones that are dehydrated, but they are still delicious and a fine addition to your raw chocolate.

COCONUT CRISPIES

You will need:
- 100 g coconut chips
- 65 g maple syrup
- 15 g coconut flour
- Pinch of salt
- 4-5 drops Medicine Flower pure vanilla flavour (or pure vanilla extract), optional, but so worth it for aroma and taste

Measure out your coconut chips. Cover them with fresh water.

And leave to soak for an hour.

Coconut chips soaking in water

While the coconut is soaking you can gather together your other ingredients.

Ingredients for Coconut Crispies

After an hour, take another bowl and a sieve, and drain the coconut chips. The soaking water is pleasant to drink or add to a smoothie.

Give the coconut chips a good squeeze with your hands. You want them to be damp, but not soggy.

Then add your other ingredients...

...including the gorgeous maple syrup!

Give it all a good mix up with your spatula or a spoon.

Coconut flour helps the maple syrup adhere to the coconut chips

Spread out the mixture on a dehydrator sheet. Don't spread it out too thin because we want it to be quite clumpy when it dries.

Allow the mixture to develop clumps

Below are the Coconut Crispies after being in the dehydrator for 12 to 18 hours.

They're really lovely and crispy.

84

If you're not going to use them straight away store them in an airtight container. This is important because it's surprising how quickly they soften with moisture from the air.

They look so pretty! They've got the pure white colour of coconut tinted with a golden caramel colour from the maple syrup. Yummy!

The Coconut Crispies will keep well in an airtight container

CHOCOLATE - COVERED COCONUT CRISPIES

Now I'm going to show you a lovely way to use your Coconut Crispies with tempered chocolate.

These are the ingredients you'll need:

CHOCOLATE COVERED COCONUT CRISPIES

- About 50 g Coconut Crispies
- 100 g cacao butter
- 50 g cacao powder
- 50 g coconut sugar
- Pinch of salt

First of all, line a plastic container with greaseproof paper. When you are ready, make 200 grams of tempered chocolate, as you've learnt to do and divide it roughly into two.

Temper your chocolate at the last minute so it's at the right temperature

Work quickly so you don't have to retemper the chocolate. You could keep the other half warm, maybe using the bain-marie, but **make sure it doesn't go above the 33 degree threshold.**

Pour a layer of liquid, tempered chocolate into the container to cover the bottom.

Tempered chocolate forms the base of these treats

Now put a good layer of Coconut Crispies on top, keeping quite a few in chunky pieces, but a mixture of sizes to keep it interesting.

Be generous with your Crispies!

Press them down a bit and cover all the chocolate.

Pour the other half of the chocolate on top.

It's quite nice to leave some of the Crispies showing.

Tempered chocolate forms the top layer as well

87

Put in the fridge for twenty minutes or so to set.

This is ready to cool in the fridge

They're ready to eat! Don't they look delicious?

Out of the fridge and nicely set

Coconut Crispies make lovely gifts

LET YOUR FOOD (er, DRINK) BE YOUR MEDICINE

Norman Hollenberg, who studied the benefits of cocoa drinking on the Kuna Indians of Panama for many years, believed that the chemical epicatechin that is found in chocolate is as important as penicillin and anaesthesia, medically. The Kuna don't get dementia, and their incidences of heart disease, stroke, cancer and diabetes are less than 10%[2].

CHOCOLATE TROUBLE!

TROUBLESHOOTING

Sometimes things can go wrong with chocolate making, especially when you're tempering. Maybe I can help.

I've made quite a few mistakes and things sometimes don't turn out the way I had expected or even hoped. This is because **I am an incorrigible experimenter!**

It's really good to make mistakes while we're chocolate making. Yes, we are using special and expensive ingredients but chocolate is so great because almost everything can be saved.

It can be re-melted or something else equally delicious created.

Remelting chocolate is often the answer

CONSIDER THIS IN ADVANCE

I ruined a batch once because I was trying to do it when my kitchen was full of other people. It's not so much of an issue with untempered chocolate but tempering does require focus.

This is why it's a good idea to see home chocolate making as *one* of two experiences –

- **An immersive experience, even meditative if you wish, where you get totally absorbed in what you are doing. It's a time when ideas flow.**
  OR
- **A sharing experience – lovely to do with children or with a friend.**

When you know what experience you want, you can prepare accordingly.

YOUR THERMOMETER IS YOUR FRIEND

With small amounts of chocolate like you are most likely to be working with at home it is harder to control the temperature.

Your thermometer is your friend. Keep it handy and keep an eye on things.

When I first started, if the chocolate hadn't melted properly I would impatiently put the heat back on and give the water a blast.

I discovered that the chocolate would quickly heat up and go way over the temperature I wanted.

Now, if my chocolate hasn't melted completely, I take the bowl off the pan, heat up the water again and then put the bowl back on, being really careful to keep an eye on the temperature.

SPECIFIC TO TEMPERED CHOCOLATE

If your chocolate gets too cool it will become too thick to work with and you will have to warm it up again.

You will need to re-heat it up really carefully on the double boiler, keeping it under 33 degrees.

If it goes over, you will have to retemper.

If you do have to retemper chocolate because you've taken it too high, don't worry because it can, in fact, create an even better chocolate.

BLOOM

There are two types of *bloom* that can occur in chocolate.

Bloom can look like this

One is caused by moisture in the chocolate and is called *sugar bloom*.

To avoid it, keep your utensils, moulds and other equipment dry. Wipe the bottom of your bowl after you remove it from the pan before you temper.

Store your chocolate carefully, cool and dry, not in the fridge. The fridge is for short periods of cooling and setting, or for untempered chocolate. Avoid any chance of the chocolate being affected by condensation.

Using the fridge - yes to short periods of setting tempered chocolate; no to storing it

The second type of bloom is called *fat bloom*. It can be caused by poor tempering or if chocolate is stored somewhere that is too warm. If it happens to your chocolate, you should be able to remedy this by retempering.

In addition, there are alternative tempering techniques and advanced tempering that you can investigate to improve your skills.

OTHER PROBLEMS WITH MOISTURE

Tempered chocolate may *seize* if you get even a small amount of moisture in while you are working with it.

The chocolate thickens and you can no longer use it for its original purpose.

You may well be able to rescue it by, funnily enough, carefully adding more liquid, turning it into *ganache*. Then, you could create some delicious truffles and all is well. Search online for ganache recipes.

Chocolate ganache

WHAT TO DO IF YOUR CHOCOLATE GETS STUCK IN THE MOULD

Occasionally tempered chocolate doesn't come out of the mould easily.

If this happens, pop it back in the fridge for a little while.

If the chocolate still refuses to come out, have a look at the underside of the mould.

If the chocolate is still completely dark in colour after 20 minutes or so, it's a sign that it hasn't contracted and it probably hasn't been tempered properly.

Put it in the freezer for a little while. It should pop out of the mould easily.

Allow it to reach room temperature. Then melt it and retemper it.

It should retemper fine so long as it's not been affected by condensation.

Chocolate that wasn't tempered well and stuck to the mould

KEEPING THINGS STEADY

As silicone moulds are flexible and wobbly, fill them on a board or small tray and put the whole thing into the fridge. If you do happen to overfill your mould, the edges of your chocolates can be trimmed with a sharp knife once they are set.

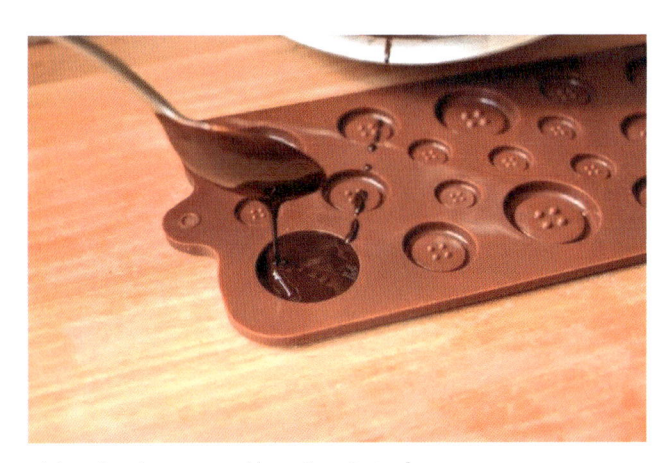

Your board can move around when chopping or shaving cacao butter. Put it on something that will stay still, like a tea towel.

A tea towel under your board can keep it steady

Good luck with your chocolate making. Practice makes perfect. And what a wonderful thing to practice – raw chocolate making!

A board under your mould can keep it steady

STORING YOUR FINISHED CHOCOLATE

Untempered chocolate can be stored in the fridge, or even the freezer. In the fridge it should keep for a few weeks. Keep it in an airtight container as chocolate can pick up and absorb strong smells.

Tempered chocolate should be kept in a container in a cool, dry place, not in the fridge. If it is well tempered and well stored, it should keep for up to a year.

USEFUL TEMPERATURES

- 50 degrees to 54 degrees Celsius – around this and above, chocolate may burn and not be any good
- 42 to 45 degrees Celsius – around this and under, chocolate is considered 'raw'
- 42 degrees Celsius – the temperature to aim for when melting chocolate that is to be tempered
- 33 degrees Celsius – chocolate comes out of temper and will need to be re-tempered
- 31.5 degrees Celsius – the temperature at which tempered chocolate is ready to work with

And lastly some ancient wisdom:

"Take time for Chocolate!"

ACKNOWLEDGEMENTS

Thank you to Mike Hewitt for editorial assistance, advice and encouragement. This book is all the richer for your input.

Thank you to Amy Levin for permission to use her recipe for Coconut Crispies (known as Candied Coconut Clusters). You can find out more about Amy at www.amylevin.co.uk.

PICTURE CREDITS

Thank you to Ken Backhouse for all his original photography, used throughout the book.

Thank you to Amy Levin for permission to use her photographs. www.amylevin.co.uk.

Thank you to Pablo Spaull for permission to use his photographs. You can find out more about Forever Cacao at www.forevercacao.co.uk.

Thank you to Pixabay for photos used. Check out their copyright free images at www.pixabay.com.

Other picture credits:

Lucuma photo by Akramm. License: Creative Commons Attribution Share Alike 3.0 Unported

Maple sugar photo by elPadawan. License: Creative Commons Attribution Share Alike 2.0 Generic

Quetxalcoatl picture by Eddo. License: Creative Commons Attribution Share Alike 3.0 Unported

Chocolate drinking vessel photo by Simon Burchell. License: Creative Commons Attribution Share Alike 3.0 Unported

Cacao glyph – public domain clipart, www.wpclipart.com

Woodcut image of cocoa tree from *Historia del Mondo Nuovo* by Girolama Benzoni, 1563. Creator anonymous

REFERENCES

[1] For example, Krittanawong et al., publishing in *The European Journal of Preventative Cardiology* in 2020, looked at a number of studies and found that compared with consuming chocolate less than once a week, eating chocolate more than once a week was associated with an 8% decreased risk of coronary artery disease.

[2] Dr Norman K Hollenberg, a renowed leader in cardiovascular medicine, studied the Kuna people of Panama to understand why their incidence of heart disease, dementia, stroke and other serious diseases were so low compared to their neighbours. He was looking to see if they had protective genes, but he discovered something else. He found that they drank high levels of natural cocoa and concluded that this was what protected them. Compounds in natural, ie low-processed, cocoa, increase blood flow to the brain, protecting the Kuna from dementia. His research found that flavanol-rich cocoa could protect against heart disease and other serious illness.

[3] For example, researchers Crozier et al, publishing in *Chemistry Central Journal* in 2011, found that chocolate has significantly higher levels of antioxidants and flavanols than fruits such as blueberries, cranberries and acai, normally considered to be 'super fruits'. They wrote that natural cocoa powder and dark chocolate should be considered 'super foods'. Study funded by Hershey Chocolate.

RECOMMENDED BOOKS

- *Naked Chocolate* by David Wolfe and Shazzie
- *Superfoods* by David Wolfe

SUE FRISBY aka CHOCOMAMA

I have been making raw chocolate professionally for many years, with my brand, *Chocomama*, and I love to show others how they can create delicious healthy treats for themselves and their loved ones.

I really enjoy showing people how to make chocolate using high quality, organic ingredients, all centred round unroasted cacao.

I am an avid experimenter and love to explore new ways of making treats that are full of vitality and taste wonderful.

Raw Chocolate Making with Chocomama is the book companion to my online video course of the same name. It is available on educational platforms, Udemy (www.udemy.com) and Skillshare (www.skillshare.com).

INDEX

additives, 31
agave, 39
Amy Levin, 22, 23, 24, 74, 98, 99
antioxidants, 1, 18, 53, 100
Asháninka, 26
bain-marie, 46, 47, 58, 71, 78, 89
bespoke chocolate, 20
bloom, 76, 93, 94
brain function, 1
buckwheaties, 27
cacao, 2, 3, 4, 6, 7, 13, 14, 15, 16, 17, 18, 20, 21, 22, 26, 30, 31, 33, 34, 47, 49, 50, 51, 52, 54, 60, 61, 62, 64, 65, 71, 72, 76, 77, 78, 95, 101
cacao bean, 15
cacao butter, 16, 17, 31, 52, 60, 61, 64, 71
cacao mass, 51
cacao paste, 51
cacao percentage, 3, 18, 33
cacao powder, 18, 51, 52, 62, 78
cacao trees, 50
candied nuts, 28
children, 6, 22, 93
chocolate cravings, 7
circulation, 1
citrus peel, 69
coconut oil, 31
coconut sugar, 14, 21, 33, 34, 35, 36, 37, 38, 52, 53, 54, 61, 62, 68, 69, 77, 78
    coconut blossom sugar, 52
    coconut palm sugar, 52
commercial chocolate, 6, 13, 16
conventional chocolate, 7, 20, 30, 31
couverture, 20, 21
criollo, 26, 52
Crozier, 100
dehydrator, 26, 27, 28, 47, 57, 69, 70, 86
double boiler, 46, 58, 71, 78, 93
emulsifiers, 16, 31
erythritol, 21, 27, 30, 36, 37
essential oils, 54, 67
fatty acids, 2
flavanols, 100
flavonoid, 69
Forever Cacao, 25, 26, 99
ganache, 8, 94
grinder, 30, 46, 61
handmade chocolate, 20

heart, 1, 16, 20, 100
heirloom, 26
Hollenberg, 100
honey, 31, 39
inclusions, 20, 27, 61, 67
ketogenic diet, 36
Krittanawong, 100
Kuna, 100
low carb, 36
lucuma, 38, 99
magnesium, 1, 17
maltitol, 30
maple sugar, 39, 99
maple syrup, 14, 27, 34, 35, 53, 62, 64, 68, 69, 71, 78, 85, 86, 87
meditative activity, 8
mesquite, 38
microplane, 69
moisture, 7, 46, 56, 72, 78, 87, 94
moulds, 44, 45, 57, 58, 66, 67, 72, 76, 82, 94
mouth feel, 76
mulberries, 21, 37, 38
natural food colours, 27
non-chocolate fat, 16, 31
nutrients, 1, 15, 16, 27, 31, 36
organic farming, 26
Pablo Spaull, 25, 26, 99
pets, 7
pink Himalayan crystal salt, 54
rainforest, 26
raw cane sugar', 35
raw food, 6, 13, 23, 26, 27
raw food diet, 6, 27
raw granola, 27
raw sweeteners, 14
retemper, 20, 89
salt, 53, 54, 62, 64, 68, 69, 71, 78, 85
saturated fat, 16
seize, 8, 94
serotonin, 1
shine, 5
silicone moulds, 44, 45, 66, 72, 95
snap, 5, 75, 76
soya, 31
soya lecithin, 31
stability, 5
stable fats, 16

stevia, 37
sugar alcohols, 30, 36
sun-dried cane juice, 35
superfood, 2, 13
sweeteners, 14, 23, 30, 35, 46
temperature, 16, 27, 46, 47, 57, 61, 72, 78, 79, 89, 93, 95
tempering, 5, 7, 14, 45, 48, 57, 72, 75, 76, 77, 79, 82, 92, 93, 94
textures, 4, 61

theobroma, 16
thermometer, 46, 57, 65, 78, 93
troubleshooting, 80
truffles, 8, 82, 94
untempered chocolate, 4, 5, 35, 37, 39, 44, 45, 53, 57, 62, 64, 65, 67, 71, 72, 76, 93, 94
vegan, 4, 6, 23, 31
xylitol, 21, 27, 30, 36, 37
yacon, 21, 38

Printed in Great Britain
by Amazon